We Make Cookies

Written by Katherine Mead

STECK-VAUGHN®
C O M P A N Y

A Division of Harcourt Brace & Company

We make cookies. One, two, three.

We mix the dough. Mix, mix, mix.

We roll the dough. Roll, roll, roll.

We cut the dough. Cut, cut, cut.

We bake the dough. Wait, wait, wait.

We frost the cookies. Fun, fun, fun.

We eat the cookies. Yum, yum, yum.